TO FREDERIK.

Hope you have a great journey to the earth core !!

:)

All my best
Dan

Dr Volcano

THIS IS A CARLTON BOOK

Published in 2019 by Carlton Books Limited
An imprint of the Carlton Publishing Group
20 Mortimer Street, London W1T 3JW

Text, design and illustration copyright
© Carlton Books Limited 2019

Design, illustration and editing: Dynamo Limited

All rights reserved. This book is sold subject to the condition that it may not be reproduced, stored in a retrieval system or transmitted in any form or by any means, electronic, mechanical, photocopying, recording or otherwise, without the publisher's prior consent.

A catalogue record for this book is available from the British Library.

ISBN: 978-1-78312-509-8
9 8 7 6 5 4 3 2 1
Printed in China

DIG TO THE CENTRE OF THE EARTH

Dougal Jerram
The Centre for Earth Evolution and Dynamics,
University of Oslo, Norway/DougalEARTH Ltd., UK

MISSION TO THE MIDDLE

Nobody has ever made a journey to the centre of the Earth. In fact, we know less about the inner workings of our planet than we know about space. This guide will give you all the information that we have, but ultimately this will be a mission into the unknown.

We know that you will be travelling through fiery hot rocks under super-heavy pressures that would normally be deadly! But your eventual destination is the biggest mystery of all. What exactly is at the core?

One thing is for certain — this adventure will be extreme.

GOOD LUCK!

INSIDE YOUR GUIDE

YOUR MISSION PLAN

8 The adventure starts here
10 Your travel vehicle
12 Time detecting
14 Earth stats
16 Earthquake alert

BEGIN YOUR JOURNEY

18 Start in space
20 The volcano route
22 The sea route
24 Tour the crust
26 Crust sightseeing

GOING DEEPER

28 Three to tick
30 Into the magma
32 Down to the edge
34 The outer core
36 The inner core
38 You've arrived!

MISSION ACCOMPLISHED

40 Getting home again
42 Question time
44 Glossary

THE ADVENTURE STARTS HERE

There are some amazing sights to see on a journey to the centre of the Earth. This book will give you all the background you need to plan your quest.

Get to know your super-powered travel pod.

Decide where to begin. Will you start by going into a volcano or diving underwater?

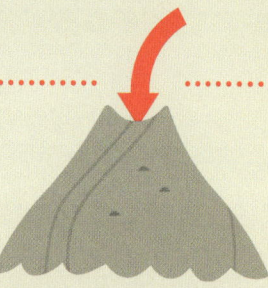

Discover the highlights you won't want to miss, including caves full of giant crystals.

Check out suggestions for things to do, such as diamond-hunting.

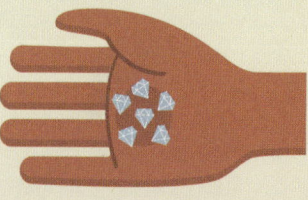

HAPPY EXPLORING

CRUST

YOUR MISSION PLAN

FROM CRUST TO CORE

You'll encounter Earth's different layers as you travel from its crust to its centre. Here's what to expect.

CRUST

The layers beneath our feet start with the crust. This can be continental (on land) or oceanic (under the ocean). It's a relatively thin layer of solid rock surrounding the planet like the shell of an egg.

MANTLE

The mantle is the next layer you will encounter on your journey. It is broadly split into two sections — the upper mantle and the lower mantle. The lower you travel in the mantle, the hotter you will find it.

CORE

Earth's core has two layers — the liquid outer core and the solid inner core. It's thought to be made of metals, mainly iron and nickel. Scientists would be very excited if you brought back a sample to confirm their ideas and theories about this mysterious centre.

CORE

LOWER MANTLE

UPPER MANTLE

70% of the crust **is underwater.**

The upper mantle can contain **FLUID ROCK CALLED *MAGMA*** and this layer can move slowly like sticky toffee.

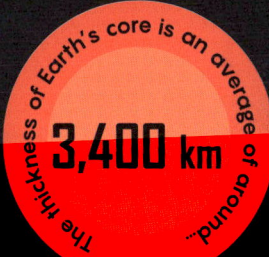
The thickness of Earth's core is an average of around... **3,400 km**

YOUR TRAVEL VEHICLE

It's not going to be easy getting to the centre of the Earth. You will need a special vehicle, and luckily we have a super-craft like no other, equipped with the very latest tunnelling technology and safety features. Meet the *GeoPod* (Geological Purpose-built Operated Driller).

GEOPOD DESIGN OBJECTIVES

Purpose of vehicle: to navigate, explore, and endure extreme conditions, and keep everyone alive.

 Establish location, depth, and co-ordinates.

 Check pressure and temperature.

 Report on the age of rocks encountered.

 Provide a comfortable home from home.

 Keep everyone onboard alive.

GEO-DRILL

ROCKET JET

The *GeoPod* has an evacuation mini-pod similar to spacecraft. It will jet you back up to Earth's surface at top speed.

YOUR MISSION PLAN

ROUTE

You can choose a route and pre-program a journey or you can drive yourself.

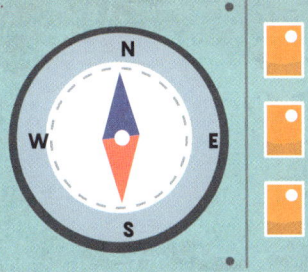

CO-ORDINATES

Program in co-ordinates if you want to visit a specific location such as the opal mines of Australia or the gold seams of America.

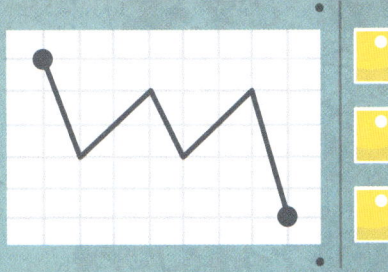

PRESSURE

TEMPERATURE

DEPTH

 POWER
 EXPERIENCE

SPEEDOMETER

SEISMOMETER

SPACE
EARTH
WATER
DRILL

GEOPOD TRAVEL SETTING

11

TIME DETECTING

Using the *GeoPod*'s instruments you can analyse rocks you pass to discover how old they are and what they tell us about Earth's history.

4.6 BILLION YEARS OLD
HAPPY BIRTHDAY

Earth began as a molten ball of material around 4.6 billion years ago. If it had been left to cool from then on, it would be a solid cold ball by now. However, some of its rocks contain radioactive elements such as uranium and thorium. They produce heat as they slowly decay through time, and they will keep the planet warm for billions of years to come.

Antarctic ice cores show how Earth's climate changes over time.

The planet has gone through very cold periods, called *ice ages*, in the past.

— SUMMER LAYER
— WINTER LAYER

CLIMATE CLUES

We know that Earth has gone through both warm periods and chilly ice ages because scientists have drilled ice cores — long plugs of ice — from modern-day Antarctica. The cores contain layers dating back 800,000 years, some of which represent very cold weather, but others contain pollen and algae from warmer times.

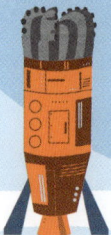

YOUR MISSION PLAN

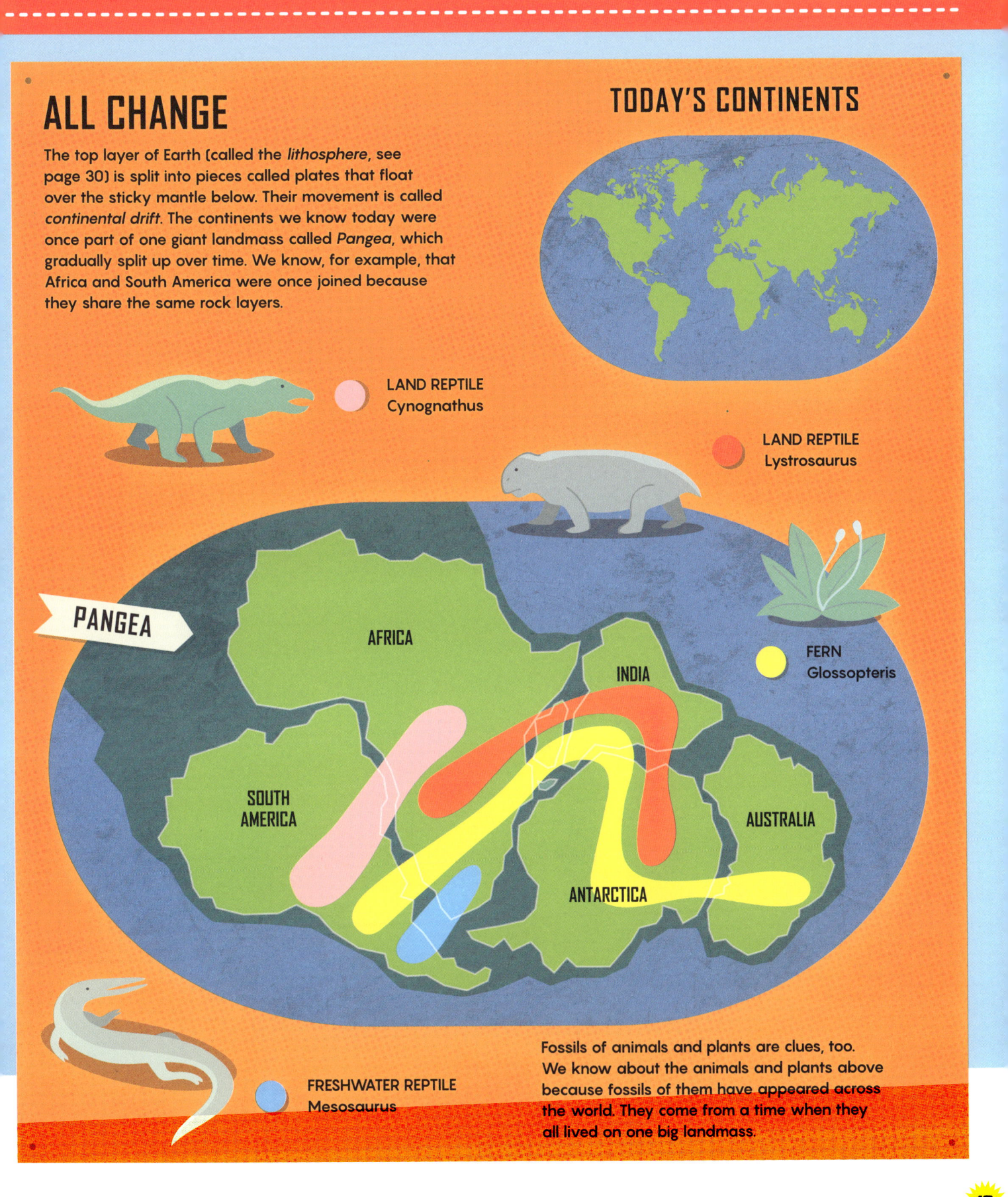

ALL CHANGE

The top layer of Earth (called the *lithosphere*, see page 30) is split into pieces called plates that float over the sticky mantle below. Their movement is called *continental drift*. The continents we know today were once part of one giant landmass called *Pangea*, which gradually split up over time. We know, for example, that Africa and South America were once joined because they share the same rock layers.

TODAY'S CONTINENTS

LAND REPTILE
Cynognathus

LAND REPTILE
Lystrosaurus

FERN
Glossopteris

PANGEA

AFRICA
INDIA
SOUTH AMERICA
ANTARCTICA
AUSTRALIA

FRESHWATER REPTILE
Mesosaurus

Fossils of animals and plants are clues, too. We know about the animals and plants above because fossils of them have appeared across the world. They come from a time when they all lived on one big landmass.

13

EARTH STATS

You'll need to know some of Earth's vital statistics to plan the trip. Here is a rundown of its most important features.

HOW DEEP IS THE PLANET?

The answer to this question is that it depends where you are. Earth isn't a perfect round shape. It's an oblate spheroid, like a grapefruit — slightly flatter at the top and bottom, and fatter round the middle (the equator).

BETWEEN 8 and 70 km
The thickness of Earth's crust, which makes up one per cent of the planet's total volume.

AVERAGE 2,886 km
The thickness of Earth's mantle, which makes up 84 per cent of the planet's total volume.

15%
The core makes up around 15 per cent of Earth's total volume.

NORTH POLE

6,357 km from the poles to the centre.

EQUATOR

6,378 km from the equator to the centre.

SOUTH POLE

YOUR MISSION PLAN

4,000 °C (7,232 °F)

Temperature at the bottom of the mantle.

HOW HOT?

Earth's temperature increases towards its centre. The temperature in the crust will vary. The oldest parts are the coolest.

6,000 °C (10,832 °F)

The inner core is about the same temperature as the surface of the sun.

FEEL THE FORCE

Rock will push down on your head with greater force as you journey to the centre. The pressure will rise until you get to the very middle, where it will be 3.65 million times higher than air pressure on the surface.

Your *GeoPod* pressure gauge will rise higher as you journey downwards. Pressure is measured in bars. As a comparison, the pressure in a car tyre is around 2 bars. At the centre, it will be 3,650,000 bars.

CAR TYRE = 2 BARS

CENTRE OF CORE = 3,650,000 BARS

EARTHQUAKE ALERT

If you choose to begin your journey by entering the mantle between two plates, be wary. You will be in an earthquake zone.

TECTONIC PLATES

The world's plates ride around on the surface of the planet, moving as the heat inside the planet circulates and slowly churns the mantle below. The map on the right shows Earth's major plates.

BEWARE EARTHQUAKES

Earthquakes occur due to pressure along the boundaries between the plates. Be careful if you begin your journey here. Although you can enter the mantle more quickly by following the line of one plate being pushed (subducted) under another, you will be in a danger zone. Thankfully the *GeoPod* can detect earthquakes occurring and take evasive action if necessary. The point on Earth's surface directly above an earthquake is called the epicentre. The *GeoPod* will map all the earthquakes as they happen. We measure the strength of earthquakes using the Richter scale — the higher the number, the stronger the earthquake.

SEISMIC WAVES

Earthquakes cause energy waves called *seismic waves* that pass through Earth. Their journeys can be measured and they have helped us understand what is inside the planet. There are two types of seismic wave, called *S waves* and *P waves*. S waves can't pass through liquid, and we know they don't pass all the way through the planet. That's how we know that there is liquid in the outer core. P waves can pass all the way through Earth but they get refracted (bent) by the inner core. That's how we know it's solid.

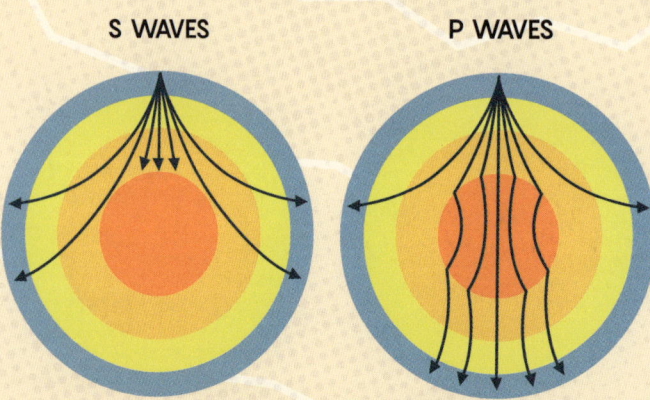

S WAVES P WAVES

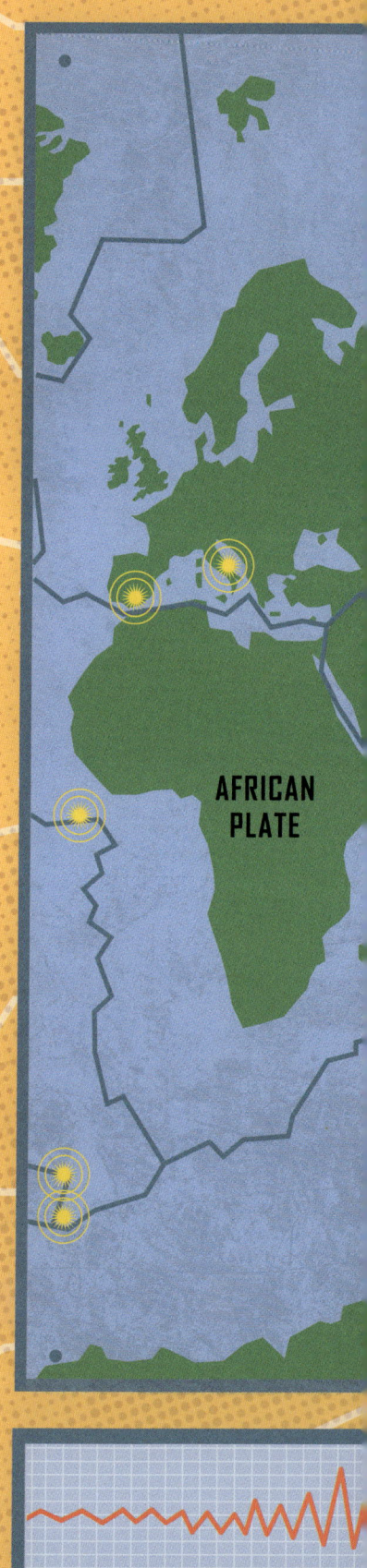

AFRICAN PLATE

START IN SPACE

If you head down to the centre of the Earth from the level where you live, you will miss out on some of the key layers in the atmosphere. These are also part of the planet and the *GeoPod* has a space setting if you'd like to explore them.

EXOSPHERE
690 to 10,000 km high.

THERMOSPHERE
85 to 690 km high.

INTERNATIONAL SPACE STATION

METEORS

MESOSPHERE
50 to 85 km high.

STRATOSPHERE
From a variable beginning up to 48 km high.

HIGH-ALTITUDE AIRCRAFT

TROPOSPHERE
Varies in thickness from around 17 km at the equator to as thin as 7 km at the poles.

18

BEGIN YOUR JOURNEY

WEATHER SATELLITE

The exosphere is the outermost layer of the atmosphere. It's where weather satellites orbit. The temperature here is very hot and there are hardly any air molecules.

The International Space Station orbits in the thermosphere. The Kármán line, at 100 km high, is where outer space is said to begin.

AURORA BOREALIS

THE KÁRMÁN LINE

The mesosphere is where most meteors turn to shooting stars as they burn up. The higher you go in the mesosphere, the colder the temperature gets.

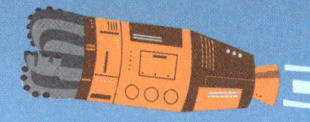

The stratosphere is where aircraft fly to avoid the weather below. It is home to the ozone layer, an area that contains a high concentration of the chemical ozone.

OZONE LAYER

WEATHER BALLOON

Most of the air molecules and water vapour in the atmosphere are found in the troposphere. Weather occurs here, as the air and water molecules move around, causing wind, clouds, and rain.

19

THE VOLCANO ROUTE

Heading down the throat of a volcano is a very direct route into the mantle and on into the centre of the Earth. The *GeoPod* is heat-proof and gas-proof. Remain inside unless you are wearing protective clothing.

INTO A LAVA LAKE

The best entry would be through a lava lake, a pool of molten lava in a volcano crater. These are constantly active, but they tend to be calm enough to allow a safe descent. Lava lakes don't often last, but here is a list of the oldest and most dramatic ones.

BUBBLING CAULDRONS OF FIR

BEGIN YOUR JOURNEY

There are solidified (cooled) lava lakes and live molten ones on Kilauea, Big Island, Hawaii. It erupted in 2018 and caused widespread damage.

The oldest lava lake in the world is inside the Erta Ale volcano in Ethiopia. Also known as the *gateway to hell*, it has two lava lake craters to choose from.

KILAUEA, HAWAII

ERTA ALE VOLCANO, ETHIOPIA

MOUNT NYIRAGONGO, DRC

VILLARRICA, CHILE

The largest lava lake in the world is in Mount Nyiragongo in the Democratic Republic of Congo. It's located in Virunga National Park, and its lake is around 670.5m (2,200 ft.) wide.

Villarrica is one of Chile's most active volcanoes. Its other name, Rucapillán means *Pillan's House* in the language of the local Mapuche people. Pillan was a powerful legendary spirit who could make disasters happen.

670.5 m wide

LAVA LAKE ALERT

Volcanic lava lakes may produce deadly clouds of gas such as sulphur dioxide. They may also suddenly spit out glowing plumes of red-hot lava.

THE SEA ROUTE

The thinnest parts of Earth's crust are under the oceans, so this would be a good fast-entry route to the core. Here you can find crust between just eight and 10 km thick.

SUGGESTED ENTRY POINT

The deepest part of the ocean is the Challenger Deep, in the Mariana Trench in the western Pacific Ocean. In this part of Earth's crust one plate is being pushed (subducted) beneath another, so the *GeoPod* could follow the fault downwards.

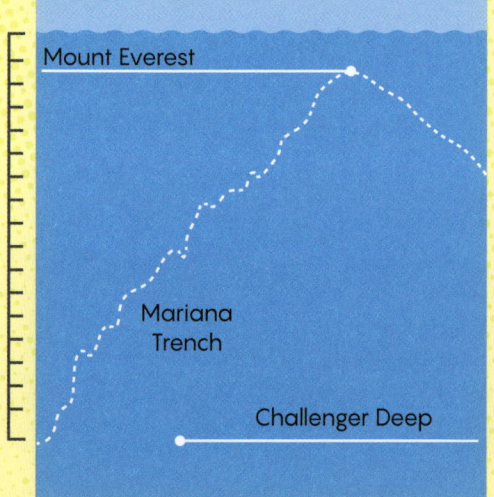

The bottom of the Challenger Deep is 11,000 m below the surface. The world's tallest mountain, Mount Everest, would fit into it comfortably, with 2,152 m of sea above it.

At this depth there is no natural light. The *GeoPod* will illuminate your surroundings.

The water pressure in the Challenger Deep is 1,000 times the pressure at sea level. But don't worry, the *GeoPod* can take it.

BEGIN YOUR JOURNEY

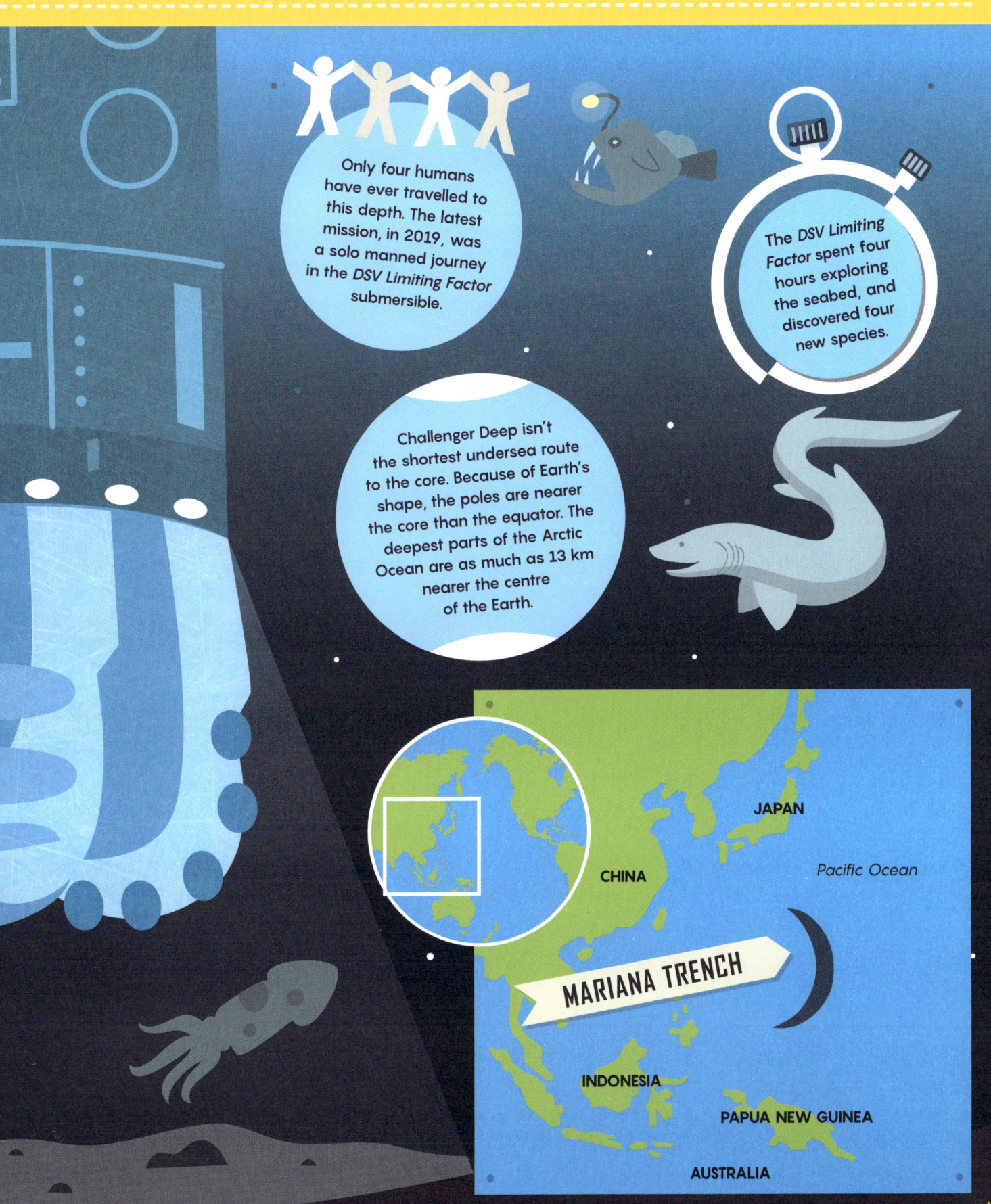

Only four humans have ever travelled to this depth. The latest mission, in 2019, was a solo manned journey in the *DSV Limiting Factor* submersible.

The *DSV Limiting Factor* spent four hours exploring the seabed, and discovered four new species.

Challenger Deep isn't the shortest undersea route to the core. Because of Earth's shape, the poles are nearer the core than the equator. The deepest parts of the Arctic Ocean are as much as 13 km nearer the centre of the Earth.

JAPAN

CHINA

Pacific Ocean

MARIANA TRENCH

INDONESIA

PAPUA NEW GUINEA

AUSTRALIA

23

TOUR THE CRUST

The crust is worth exploring before you take the plunge further down. Check the *GeoPod*'s information bank to help you.

CRINKLY CRUST

Earth's crust is split into the continental crust that we walk on and the oceanic crust beneath the seas. It's made up of rocks and contains all the various precious metals that we mine.

The crust crinkles and buckles as the super-hot interior swirls about like the inside of a lava lamp. These movements build up mountains, create valleys and plains, and feed volcanoes.

The crust makes up less than one per cent of Earth's volume.

1%

Chimborazo is 6,384 km from Earth's core.

THE LONG WAY

If you decide to take the longest route to Earth's centre, you'll need to go near to the equator, where Earth is at its fattest. Aim for the summit of the Chimborazo volcano in Ecuador, the furthest point from the core.

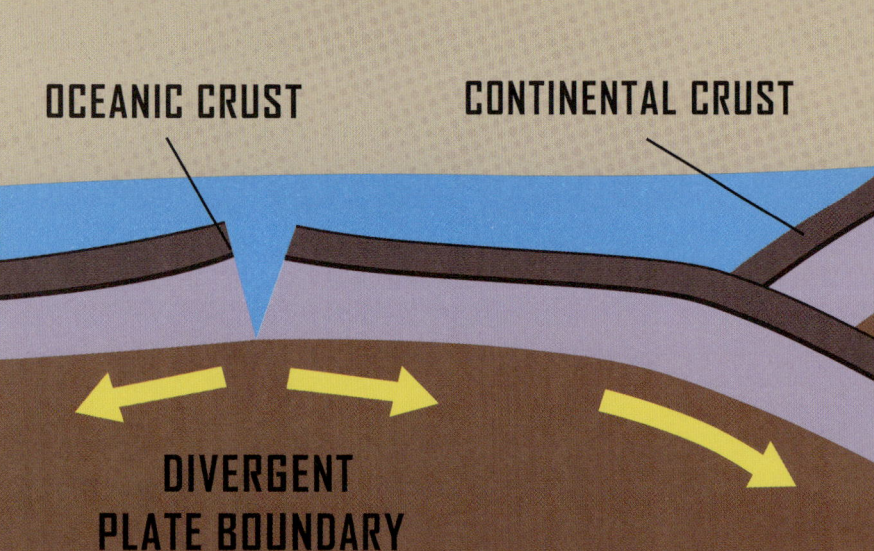

OCEANIC CRUST

CONTINENTAL CRUST

DIVERGENT PLATE BOUNDARY (OCEANIC RIFT)
A good example is the Mid-Atlantic Ridge

CONVERGENT PLATE BOUNDARY

Plate boundaries where one crust plate is being pushed under another are called *convergent plate boundaries*. Mountains are pushed up as the plates push together. The Andes Mountains in South America are an example.

BEGIN YOUR JOURNEY

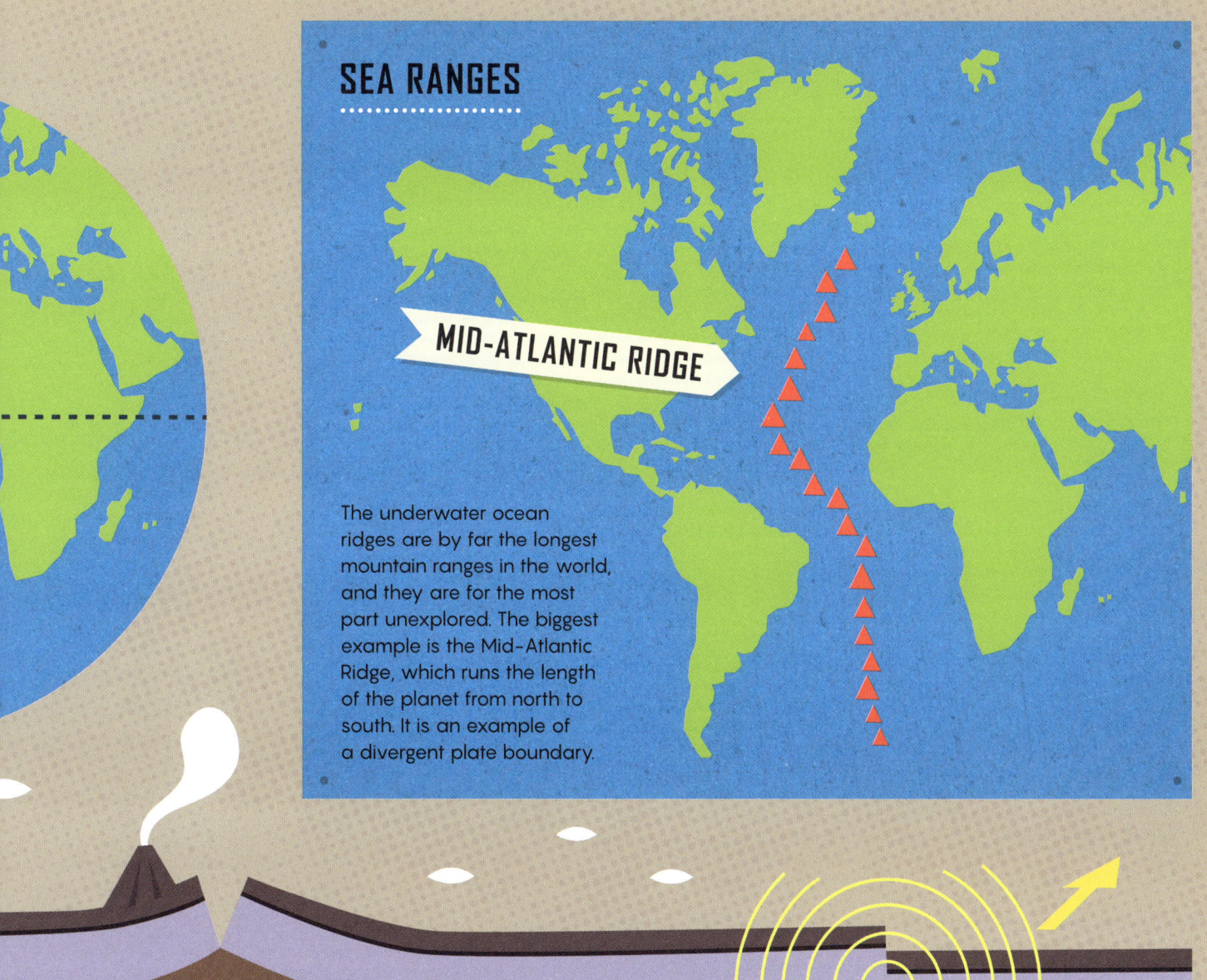

SEA RANGES

MID-ATLANTIC RIDGE

The underwater ocean ridges are by far the longest mountain ranges in the world, and they are for the most part unexplored. The biggest example is the Mid-Atlantic Ridge, which runs the length of the planet from north to south. It is an example of a divergent plate boundary.

DIVERGENT PLATE BOUNDARY
(CONTINENTAL RIFT)

Plate boundaries where the crust is moving apart are called *divergent plate boundaries*, or *rifts*. The East African Great Rift Valley is a famous example. Volcanoes are common here.

TRANSFORM PLATE BOUNDARY

When plates run side-by-side on the crust they are called *transform plate boundaries*. The San Andreas Fault around San Francisco, USA, is an example. Earthquakes often occur in these areas.

25

CRUST SIGHTSEEING

Here are some crust highlights for you to plan into your trip.

FOSSIL HUNTING

Fossils survive in sedimentary rock — sediment laid down over millions of years that has hardened into rock. The *GeoPod* will locate this rock for you and tell you which time zone it represents. Then you'll know which creatures and plants to look out for.

The most common fossils to find are marine fossils such as shells, curly ammonites, shark's teeth and trilobites, which look like big woodlice.

AMMONITE

TRILOBITE

SHARK'S TOOTH

Dinosaurs are the rarest fossils to find. Look out for large bones or fossil footprints.

DINOSAUR FOSSIL

BEGIN YOUR JOURNEY

CAVES

Find limestone rock to locate interlinking cave systems carved out by running water. More unusually, you may find lava tubes in volcano areas. These are caverns inside cooled solidified lava.

The most spectacular cave of all is the Cave of the Crystals in Mexico, found below a silver mine. Here giant crystals of gypsum up to 13 m high criss-cross the cave, which were created when underground liquid was volcanically heated.

WATER-FILLED CAVES

CRYSTAL CAVES

GEYSERS

Geysers are hot springs where boiling water and steam gush up to Earth's surface. They are created when an underground water source is heated by volcanic activity. The water is forced up by pressure and spurts out like a fountain.

PLACES TO SEE THE WORLD'S BEST GEYSERS

ICELAND — the Great Geysir and Strokkur Geysir.

USA — Old Faithful and Steamboat in Yellowstone Park.

CHILE — the El Tatio geyser field

RUSSIA — the Valley of Geysers

NEW ZEALAND — Taupo volcanic zone

THREE TO TICK

Be sure to check off these three underground experiences as you begin to explore deeper.

I PASSED THE LITHOSPHERE

The lithosphere is the name given to the crust and upper mantle, which rests on top of the deeper mantle below. It's the part of Earth involved in the slow movement of plates. Its thickness varies. At the base of the lithosphere there is a zone of partially molten rock.

I SAW THE MOHO

The *moho* is a special layer that lies around seven to 35 km below Earth's surface, in the lithosphere. It's the area where the crust and the mantle join. Under increased pressure the rocks become denser here.

Scientists have worked out where the moho is by measuring seismic waves (see page 16). They travel faster through the moho than the crust.

OCEANIC CRUST

CONTINENTAL CRUST

MOHO

LITHOSPHERE

UPPER MANTLE (THE ROCKS ARE RIGID HERE, BUT DENSE)

UPPER MANTLE (SLOWLY FLOWING)

GOING DEEPER

I HUNTED FOR DIAMONDS

As you travel through the lithospheric mantle (the upper part of the mantle attached to the crust), take a detour to areas beneath the oldest part of the crust, known as cratons. Look for very high pressures and temperatures at around 140 to 300 km down to give yourself a good chance of finding diamonds!

KIMBERLITES

Diamonds are brought to the surface in eruptions through volcanic tubes called kimberlites. The material comes from deep underground.

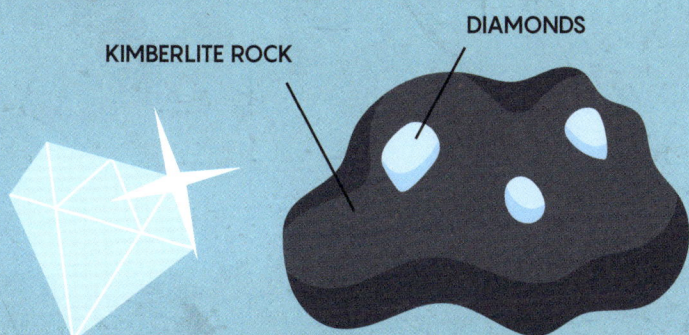

KIMBERLITE ROCK

DIAMONDS

The top of a kimberlite pipe, where diamonds are mined.

CRATONS WHERE DIAMONDS ARE LOCATED:

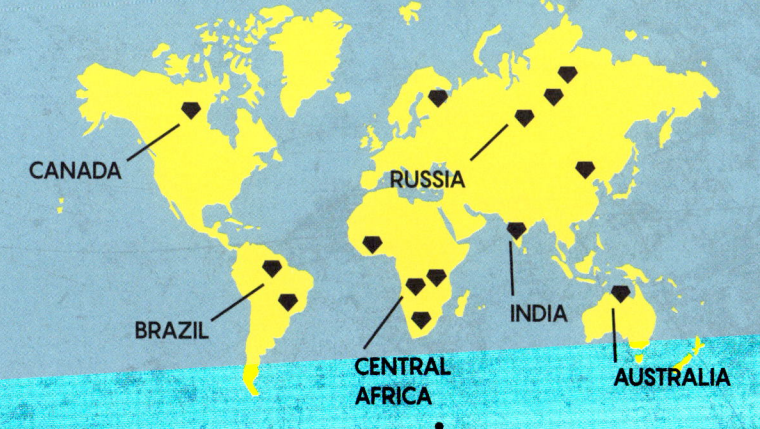

CANADA

BRAZIL

RUSSIA

CENTRAL AFRICA

INDIA

AUSTRALIA

29

INTO THE MAGMA

The mantle layer is found beneath the crust. It is by far the largest layer and you will spend most of your journey time there. What should you expect?

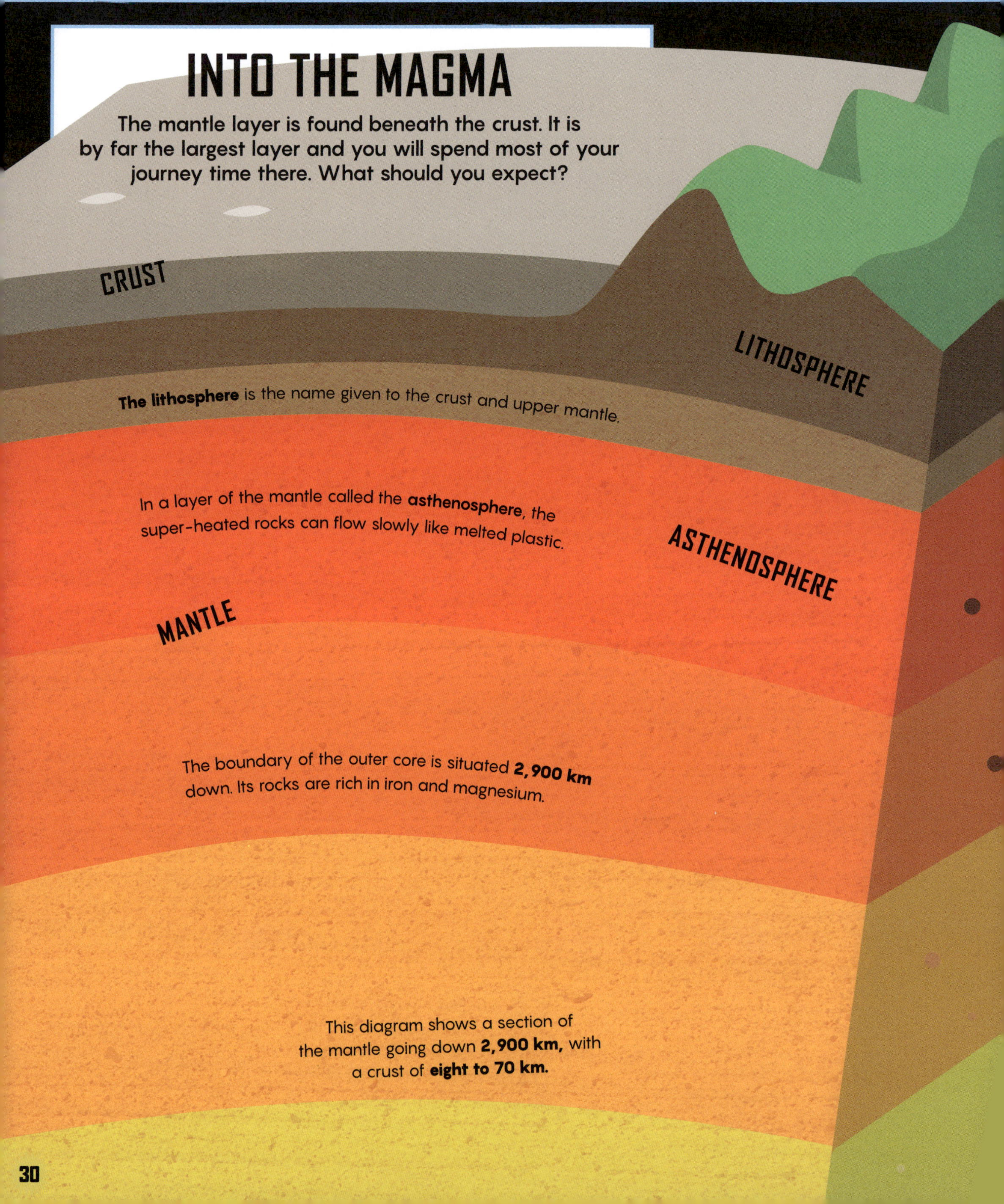

CRUST

LITHOSPHERE

The lithosphere is the name given to the crust and upper mantle.

In a layer of the mantle called the **asthenosphere**, the super-heated rocks can flow slowly like melted plastic.

ASTHENOSPHERE

MANTLE

The boundary of the outer core is situated **2,900 km** down. Its rocks are rich in iron and magnesium.

This diagram shows a section of the mantle going down **2,900 km**, with a crust of **eight to 70 km**.

GOING DEEPER

TRAVEL WARNING

Within the upper mantle there are pockets of liquid rock called magma. It gathers in chambers beneath the crust, but can erupt under pressure out of vents such as volcanoes and undersea fault lines.

When it reaches the surface it cools as lava. If the *GeoPod* hits one of these magma chambers, prepare for a bumpy ride! The *GeoPod* computer will give you instructions on what to expect.

HIDDEN MAGMA CHAMBER

EMERGENCY INFORMATION: MAGMA CHAMBERS

If you hit a magma chamber by mistake, you will feel turbulence in the *GeoPod*, as though you were in an aircraft during stormy weather.

Relax. People have drilled into magma chambers before with no ill effects. Scientists have experimented by drilling under lava lakes. In Iceland, engineers looking for geothermal energy accidentally drilled into a magma chamber. Their drilling equipment was destroyed, but there was no disaster.

The magma in a chamber will look like a fiery glowing ocean. We know this from lava lakes that sometimes gather in the bowl of an erupting volcano. As magma cools, parts of the surface become volcanic rock, but it's still possible to see liquid rock churning and glowing between the cracks.

DOWN TO THE EDGE

As you travel down through the mantle, look out for huge rising plumes of material. Then get ready to surf along the edge of the outer core.

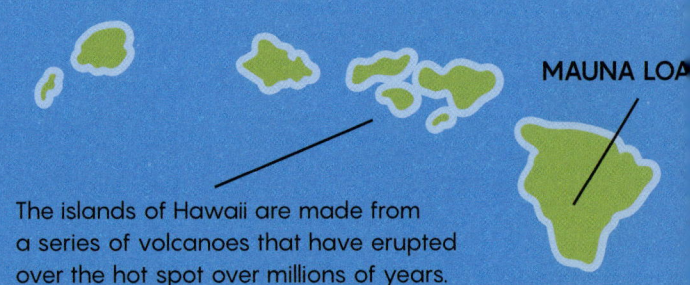

The islands of Hawaii are made from a series of volcanoes that have erupted over the hot spot over millions of years.

HAWAIIAN ISLANDS — MAUNA LOA — HOT SPOT — MANTLE PLUME

HOT-SPOTTING PLUMES

On your trip through the mantle you may see plumes — areas where an unusual amount of heat is making material rise slowly from deep within the planet, sometimes as deep as the boundary between the core and the mantle. The rock moves up and melts at the top of the plume, making the crust above into an area of volcanic activity called a hot spot.

There's a rising plume underneath Hawaii, which created Mauna Loa, one of the world's biggest volcanoes.

WORLD LOCATIONS THOUGHT TO BE HOT SPOTS:

- ICELAND
- YELLOWSTONE PARK, USA
- AFAR REGION, EAST AFRICA
- HAWAII
- PITCAIRN ISLAND
- GALÁPAGOS ISLANDS

GOING DEEPER

AT THE BOUNDARY

The boundary between the mantle and the outer core is a mysterious and fascinating place. It's called the CMB — the core-mantle boundary — and it's where the mantle's solid rocks rub up against liquid material rich in iron and nickel metals.

THE CORE-MANTLE BOUNDARY

Scientists aren't exactly sure what it looks like or what exactly happens here. You may be able to surf the surface of the churning liquid in the *GeoPod* and come back with some vital new information.

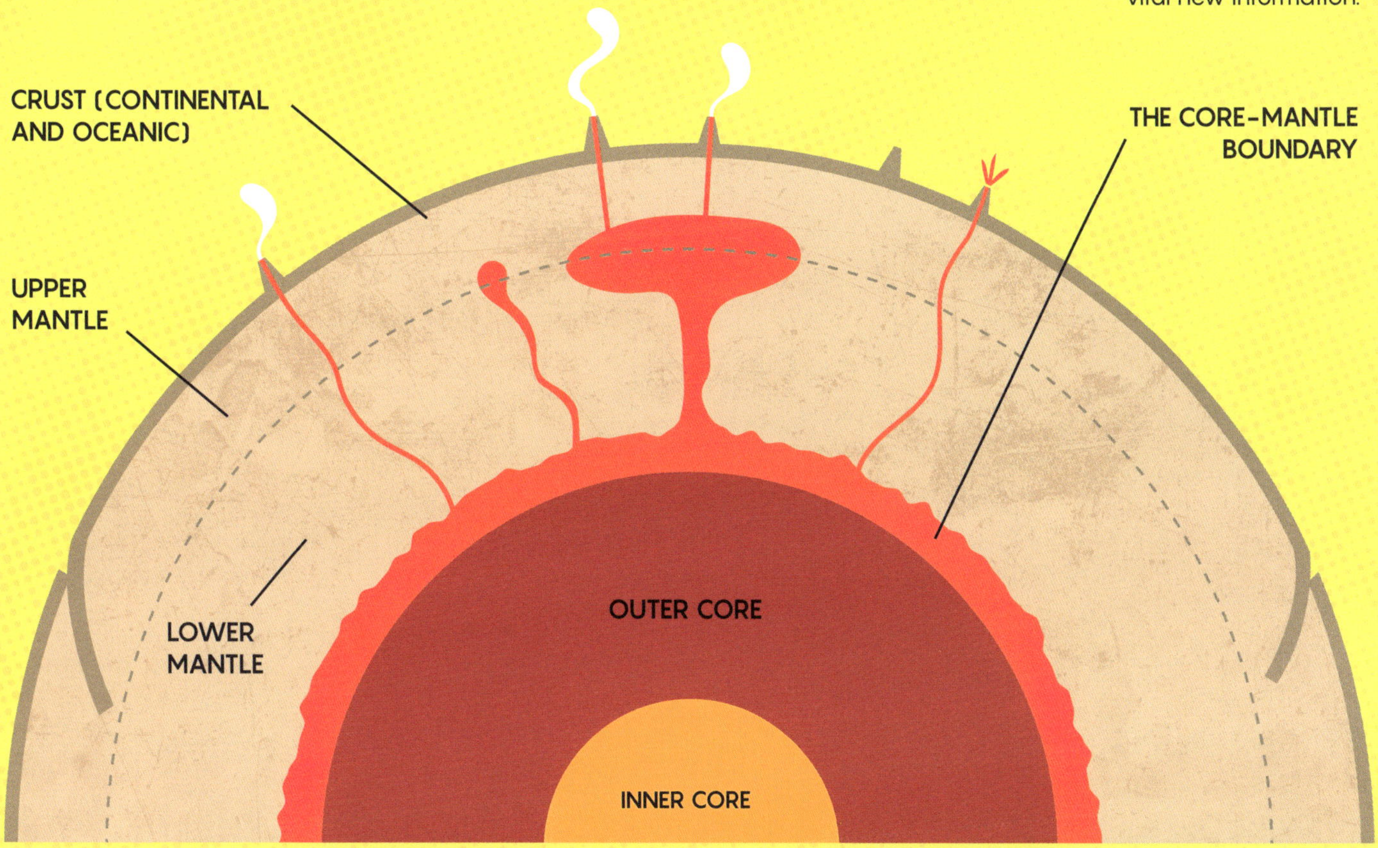

CRUST (CONTINENTAL AND OCEANIC)

UPPER MANTLE

LOWER MANTLE

THE CORE-MANTLE BOUNDARY

OUTER CORE

INNER CORE

THE OUTER CORE

When you reach the outer core, things will really heat up. The *GeoPod* will give you all the stats you need, and keep you safe.

The metals in the outer core are thought to have sunk down from the surface when Earth was young.

The outer core is liquid metal, swirling above the solid metal inner core.

As well as iron and nickel there are likely to be traces of other metals, such as gold and platinum.

The outer core is on the move, like an ocean. The *GeoPod* may be carried along by the flowing metal.

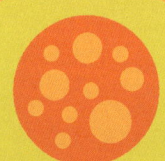

Although the core is slightly wider than the mantle it is much denser.

34

GOING DEEPER

SWAPPING POLES

Earth is surrounded by a magnetic field, with north at the North Pole and south at the South Pole. It's thought that movement within the core generates electrical currents that help create the magnetic field. Roughly every 200,000 years, this movement causes the poles to swap round. We know from magnetic minerals found in rocks that this last occurred around 780,000 years ago — so we might expect a change soon!

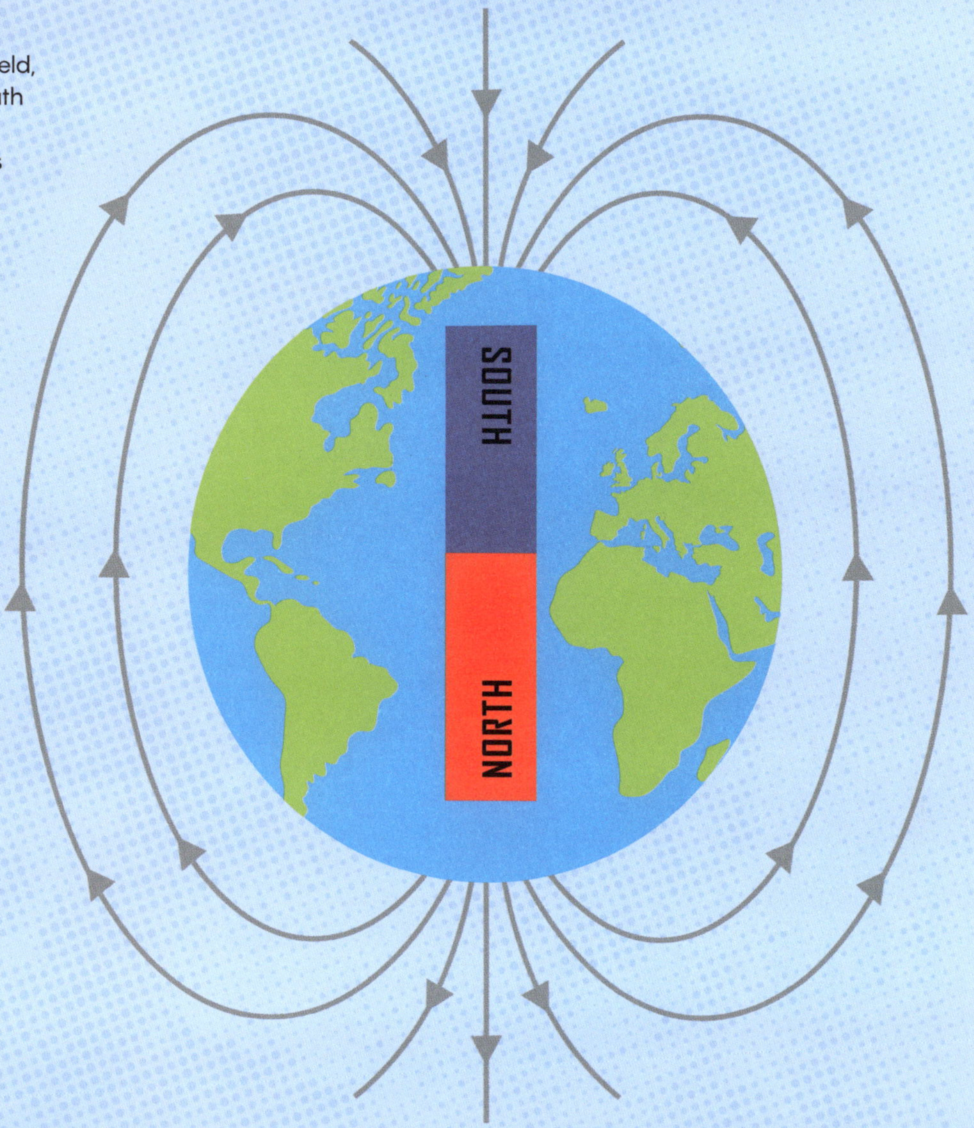

If pole-swapping occurred, a needle on a compass would start pointing south, not north.

THE INNER CORE

Once you reach Earth's centre, the *GeoPod* will need to use all its super-drilling power because the inner core is solid metal. It will be like drilling through a huge wall of hot iron.

HOW IT WAS FORMED

It's thought that around 1.5 billion years ago Earth had an unbelievably hot liquid core that was gradually cooling. When part of it solidified it sank to the centre, creating the core.

AVERAGE 2,440km
The width of the inner core.

HOW WE KNOW

Scientists have estimated the contents of the inner core by recreating its temperature (as hot as the sun's surface) and pressure (3.6 million times greater than on Earth's surface). Then they mixed materials to find out how they reacted and what the core was likely to contain.

INNER CORE RECIPE

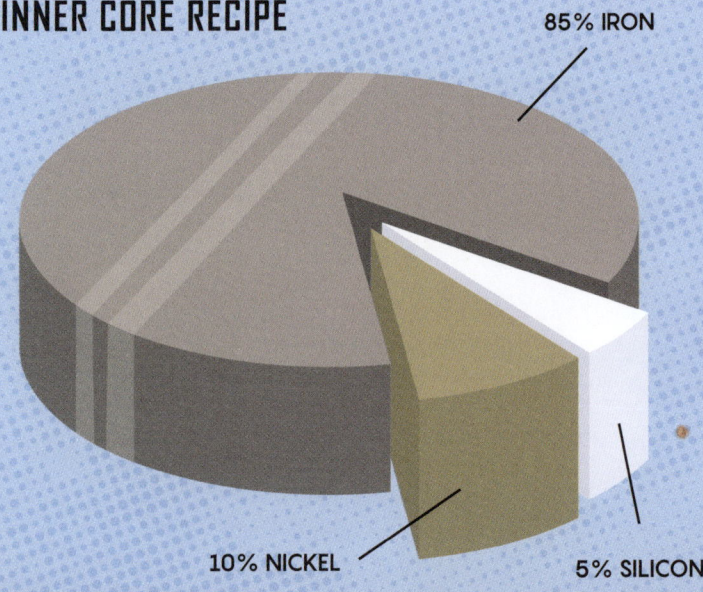

85% IRON
10% NICKEL
5% SILICON

The measurements of the inner core have been estimated by studying the speed and direction of seismic waves that pass through the planet when there are earthquakes (see page 16).

GOING DEEPER

HIDDEN WORLDS INSIDE

There have been lots of different theories about the centre of the Earth. In the 1800s an eccentric American called John Symmes persuaded many people that the centre of the Earth was hollow, open at the poles and filled with smaller hollow balls that had their own weather, and could be lived in. He tried to organise an expedition to the North Pole to journey down into the supposed hole to the middle.

This shows how a hollow Earth could look.

In Jules Verne's book *Journey to the Centre of the Earth* adventurers find dinosaurs living inside the planet.

YOU'VE ARRIVED!

At some point the *GeoPod* will shudder to a halt and buzz like a vibrating phone. Why? Because you've reached your destination! Please familiarize yourself with what to expect.

 The *GeoPod*'s dials will light up and its red beacon will flash. You will hear a voice.

"WELCOME TO THE CENTRE OF THE EARTH. WE HOPE YOU HAVE ENJOYED YOUR TRIP."

DISCOVER FOR YOURSELF

Switch to INNER CORE EXPERIENCE to experience the sounds, smells and sights outside the *GeoPod*. Will it be utterly silent or not? Let us know when you return.

SOUND

SMELL

SIGHTS

EXPERIENCE

NOTES

PRESSURE

POWER EXPERIENCE

SPEEDOMETER

SPACE
EARTH
WATER
DRILL

GEOPOD TRAVEL SETTING

GOING DEEPER

 Don't panic if you see the ship's compass swirling wildly. Down here Earth's magnetic field is not the same as it is on the surface.

 Reprogram the *GeoPod* for your return journey, deciding which route to take (see page 40 for ideas).

SAFETY GUARANTEE

The *GeoPod* will protect you from the incredible pressure and heat at the centre of the Earth. Without this super-advanced technology you would be instantly obliterated.

④ The *GeoPod* will print out a summary of your journey, with speed and distance stats and locations you have visited.

WARNING.

We are not responsible for passengers who press buttons they shouldn't.

Please see Terms and Conditions.

39

GETTING HOME AGAIN

Here are some suggestions for your return journey. Simply program the *GeoPod* for your preferred option.

MANTLE PLUME PROGRAM

Take advantage of the internal movements inside the mantle and get home quickly by riding up a plume of rising rock to one of Earth's hot spots (see page 32). Going this way you will exit via a volcano.

If you go this way, you will see beautiful blobs and shapes created in the swirling mantle plume. It will be like rising up inside a lava lamp!

MISSION ACCOMPLISHED

ANTIPODE PROGRAM

You could decide to go to the exact opposite spot to where you live, for more sightseeing. The location directly opposite another location on Earth is called its antipode. However, only 15 per cent of Earth's land is antipodal to other land. Most of it is opposite ocean. If this is where you choose, we will have a submersible ready to pick you up.

Other antipodal routes:

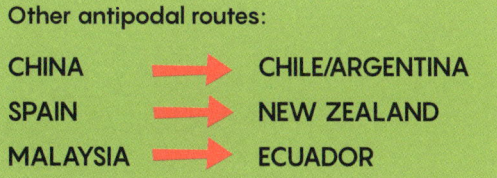

CHINA → CHILE/ARGENTINA
SPAIN → NEW ZEALAND
MALAYSIA → ECUADOR

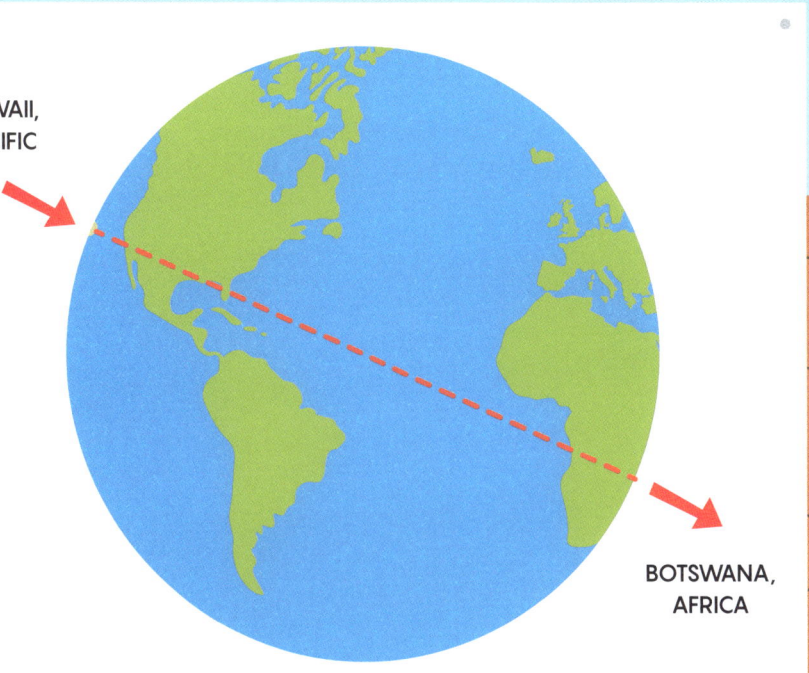

HAWAII, PACIFIC

BOTSWANA, AFRICA

LANDMARK PROGRAM

You might decide to exit via a favourite landmark or natural feature such as a mountain, giant waterfall or desert. An interesting choice would be the Grand Canyon, one of the world's most spectacular gorges. As you tunnel up, you would see layers of rocks built up over billions of years. You would be completing your trip with a unique close-up view of rocks in Earth's crust.

41

QUESTION TIME

The information we know about the centre of our planet comes from the painstaking work of brilliant scientists. They are still trying to come up with answers. Your journey will help!

THE MAN WHO CRACKED THE CORE

In 1906, British geologist Richard Dixon Oldham studied how seismic waves from earthquakes passed through Earth, and realized that they were being deflected (bent) by something dense in the middle of the planet. He had discovered Earth's core.

THE DANE WHO DID THE DOUBLE

In the 1930s, Danish scientist Inge Lehmann studied data collected from a New Zealand earthquake. By looking at the way that the seismic waves were being deflected as they travelled, she discovered that the core was made of solid and liquid areas.

IS SPACE THE SAME?

By learning more about our own planet we can more accurately predict what other planets might be like. Here are some conclusions scientists have suggested.

MERCURY
84% SOLID CORE

VENUS
MAY HAVE A LIQUID CORE

MISSION ACCOMPLISHED

THE HEAT IS ON

In 2013 French scientists tested the melting point of pure iron and produced the best estimate so far of the temperature in the centre of the Earth.

Using advanced X-ray techniques they discovered that the core was likely to be much hotter than previously thought, and this helped explain Earth's magnetic field. It's the big difference between the heat of the core and the mantle that causes material to move inside the planet. This movement, along with the spinning of the planet itself, creates the magnetic field.

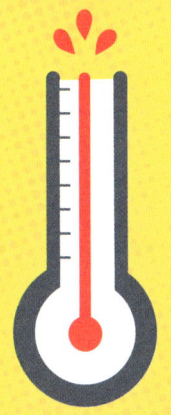

UNANSWERED

 We don't know exactly how Earth's magnetic field is affected by heat flowing through the core.

 We don't know exactly what structures (e.g. plumes) are inside the mantle. Our current maps become fuzzy as we go deeper.

 We don't know exactly when Earth's magnetic poles are likely to swap around.

MARS
MIGHT HAVE A LIQUID CORE

JUPITER
MAY HAVE A ROCK CORE

SATURN
MAY HAVE A ROCK CORE

GLOSSARY

ASTHENOSPHERE
A layer of the mantle where super-heated rock flows like melted plastic.

CONTINENTAL DRIFT
The movement of the Earth's plates.

CORE
Earth's centre.

CRATON
The name given to the oldest parts of the Earth's crust.

CRUST
A layer of rock that spreads over the surface of the planet. Continental crust is on land. Oceanic crust is underwater.

EARTHQUAKE
When the Earth's plates shift, causing changes in the crust.

EPICENTRE
The spot on the Earth's surface directly above an earthquake.

EQUATOR
An imaginary line around the middle of the Earth.

FAULT LINE
Where two of the Earth's plates meet.

GEYSER
A column of boiling water that shoots up from beneath the Earth's surface after being heated by molten rock.

HOT SPOT
A spot on the Earth's surface above a great rising plume of molten rock.

KIMBERLITE
A tube of lava that comes from deep underground, often bringing diamonds with it.

GLOSSARY

LAVA
Liquid rock flowing to the surface of the Earth.

LITHOSPHERE
The name given to the crust and upper mantle.

MAGMA
Liquid rock under the surface of the Earth.

MANTLE
A large section between Earth's crust and its core.

MARIANA TRENCH
The deepest part of the oceans, in the Pacific.

MOHO
The area where the crust and mantle join.

OBLATE SPHEROID
The shape of the planet — round but slightly flattened on the top and bottom.

PANGEA
The name given to the world's land when it was all one landmass.

PLATE
A section of the Earth's crust.

PLUME
A giant rising column of liquid rock in the mantle layer beneath the Earth's surface.

SEISMIC WAVES
Energy waves caused by earthquakes. They pass through the Earth and can be measured.

SUBDUCTED
When one plate slides under another in the Earth's crust.

VOLCANO
A vent in the Earth's crust through which lava flows.